Memorial Park

Revisiting Vietnam

Minh Nguyen

Art Metropole
Wendy's Subway

Contents

Note

Vietnamese names and proper nouns appear with or without diacritics and in first-or-last name order based on their common usage in English, or individual preferences. Ho Chi Minh City and Saigon are used interchangeably throughout, reflecting colloquial convention.

Preface

"The young woman poses for the photographer on the low wall of the esplanade above the sea, with racing clouds as a backdrop. The young woman loves the camera, and the camera loves her. She's a Vietnamese Marilyn, wrinkling her nose, giggling and tugging at her skirt."

The beauty icon described in this gushing 1989 *LA Times* profile was none other than Phan Thị Kim Phúc, popularly known as "Napalm Girl." In 1972, she had been photographed naked, screaming, her nine-year-old skin burning with napalm, and had quickly become the face of the Vietnam War's unspeakable civilian toll. Seventeen years and countless medical interventions later, Kim Phúc, now a born-again Christian, was back to assuage the collective American conscience, as if to say that nothing they had done was irredeemable. "The agonizingly wounded child had grown into a beautiful young woman," the reportage concludes, driving the point home: "not a crippled, embittered war victim."

In 1996, a year after my parents and I emigrated from Vietnam to the United States, our Marilyn was the keynote speaker at a Veterans Day commemoration in DC. "Even if I could talk face to face with the pilot who dropped the bombs," she said, "I would tell him we cannot change history, but we should try to do good things for the present and for the future to promote peace." That speech, and our arrival, were both markers of normalization between Vietnam and the US; the markets opened up to each other for the first time, remaining so until the 2025 tariffs.

Even then, something about Kim Phúc's rebrand felt hauntingly unassimilable to me; regular people, like my parents, could not normalize the history they had experienced.

My father had been drafted to fight for the US-backed Southern government. After its fall in 1975, he was captured by Northern forces and sent to a re-education camp without a stated release date, freed seven years later. Blacklisted and unable to work, my parents applied for US immigration when I was born. By the time we were approved six years later, they were, like most Vietnamese Americans, anti-Communists.

I'll never get over the randomness of where immigrants end up in the United States—how chance determines whether one lands in Los Angeles or Gainesville, Georgia. We ended up in Washington State, not far from where *Twin Peaks* was filmed, an ambivalent middle ground that could have been better but also much worse.

There is nothing quite like the alchemy of American assimilation. I seemed to learn English overnight, my accent soon undetectable. Before long, it supplanted my birth language, first in my thoughts then in my dreams. Along the way, I assimilated a generic explanation for our displacement. *We were here because of a war. War is hell but it happens sometimes. Many people die, while others, like Kim Phúc, end up triumphing over circumstance.* This story was as vague as it was powerful. I repeated it in college application essays and to American friends, but never without a certain diffuse nausea. All that carnage had to mean more than the solemn pageantry of commemoration.

By my early twenties, I had learned the progressive view on most things except for my family's history. Then, one day, I came across an ad on Tumblr for a program in Oakland called Hai Bà Trưng School for Organizing, named after two women who led the anticolonial resistance against China—an intensive multiday program geared toward "developing a base of progressive Vietnamese American organizers and activists."

There were about twenty of us from across the US—writers, teachers, public health workers—some from cities with sizable diasporas, the rest unduly excited to be among their own. The syllabus seemed designed to gently disabuse people like me of their parents' mythologies. One workshop description on the organizing methods of the Việt Minh anticipated surprise at even an ambivalent mention of communist forces: "Regardless of our individual perspectives on the Việt Minh, they successfully built a mass-based armed movement that overthrew the French."

I didn't know the first thing about the Vietnamese resistance. By the end of the course, we had covered everything from the expulsion of the French to the 1966 demonstration in Huế, when students burned down the US Consulate. Before that week in Oakland, I had understood diaspora as a private feeling, a place of angst. It was the first time I recognized that it could be a collective, mobilizing identity.

The workshops were heavy—it wasn't unusual for one of us to break down in tears—but they also had the allure of illicit knowledge. These perspectives were anathema to many of our communities. In one session, we discussed a recent dispute around the exhibition of a single photograph at a Vietnamese cultural center in Orange County. The photo depicted a woman wearing a red top with a yellow star, the current flag of the Communist Party, gazing at a bust of Hồ Chí Minh. This potentially favorable depiction of the Party ignited protests among the local community, with demonstrators surrounding the venue, vandalizing the photograph, demanding the closure of the show, and harassing all involved. An instructor played us a voicemail that a Vietnamese veteran had left one of the curators, threatening rape and murder.

The call shocked us. This was an, albeit unhinged, expression of the dominant worldview in our community. To our parents, communism is not a political theory; it's the regime that ruined their lives. They had felt the sharp edge of the system intimately. Haunted by the faces of those who had tortured them, the colonial forces that had introduced this mass violence to Vietnam were at most an abstraction.

After Oakland, the ordinary details of my family life appeared in a different light. One day, I found a piece of immigration paperwork while helping my parents clean their house. The particular legal phrasing—"US Refugee Aid"—cut to the heart of my prior uneasiness. The Americans had ravaged our country, and now we were sickeningly grateful to them.

I began questioning what I didn't know and why. A maddening process, necessarily: why had this all been kept from me? Along the way, I may have over-corrected—idealizing not only the radical forces that had expelled our colonial aggressors but also the regime that followed. In retrospect, such a romantic view was only possible at a distance.

When I made my first adult visits to Vietnam in 2017, I arrived proud to be in a socialist republic and eager to embrace the legacy conserved in the country's monuments, museums, and mausoleums. It didn't take me long to understand why people sometimes throw in the qualifier *nominally* when describing Vietnam as a communist nation. Though the ruling Communist Party brands itself as a natural outgrowth of the revolutionary period, its policies have long represented an extreme departure from the old Marxist-Leninist line. Only the capital-friendly aspects of the old regime have been maintained—particularly its apparatus of repression. Drawing on my learning curve, this collection combines travel writing and criticism to tease out the subtle contradictions at the heart of market socialism: how they resonate in art, censorship, real estate, and even my relationships.

This book goes off to the printers shortly after the fiftieth anniversary of the US defeat in Vietnam. Every interest group has a different name for April 30th. Party officials celebrated by flying ten thousand drones over the Saigon River. Exile communities, meanwhile, commemorated "The Fall of Saigon" or "Black April" by mourning in black attire. The following essays are an attempt to find out what's left of the revolution—and offer a few frank glimpses of a country whose history has been obfuscated by romantics and reactionaries alike.

Red City Smart City

I'm stuck in Smart City, a futuristic luxury complex thirty minutes outside of Hanoi. The digital keypad to my studio has malfunctioned, and the door it governs seems to have forgotten it's a door, effectively locking me inside. I press down the handle but it no longer latches onto anything solid, so I start jerking it violently and smacking the door. The phone receptionist sends up two maintenance workers. I'm relieved by their swift arrival, until they too start feebly jerking the handle from the other side. One of them slots a tool through the doorway crack. When the far edge emerges on my end, I see that it's a supermarket rewards card. They end up calling an engineer from Vinhomes, the company that owns Smart City and its proprietary technology. The man arrives after two hours and doesn't study the problem. He simply replaces the keypad. Reminded of its identity, the door pops open.

Released from my enclosure, I walk around the premises in a daze. Every skyscraper is identical to the next, like a rendering come to life. Residential units are stacked on top of ground-level businesses, barbers, mini-marts, restaurants, specialty shops for underwear and bedding. The idea of Smart City is that you never have to leave. For exercise, I can cross from one tower to the next to run in place on a conveyor belt. If I get hungry, I can purchase a single plastic-wrapped eggplant to sauté on the single-plate inductor stove in my unit. For a little natural reprieve, I can walk along a placid lake on the esplanade.

Vinhomes, the company behind Smart City, derives this comprehensive approach to integrated services from the ethos of its parent company. Vingroup, Vietnam's predominant national conglomerate, aims to cater to all human needs with its so-called "cradle-to-grave" model. The famous Vin logo, almost as omnipresent as the national flag, can be found on hospitals, supermarkets, schools, and cars. Upwardly mobile Vietnamese can drive their children to VinSchool, their young adults to VinU, and their ailing parents to Vinmec Hospital, swing by the Vincom Center for Contemporary Art on the way to their Vinhome, and do all that in a VinFast electric car.

This centralization was achieved not by the Communist Party but by the country's first billionaire, Vingroup's founder Phạm Nhật Vượng. His company is a perfect emblem for postsocialist Vietnam—softening the radical departure into corporate communism. Smart City is one of the sharpest points of this bait and switch. Superficially its model of centralized living harkens back to the famous socialist housing projects built in the 1950s, even as its function represents a perfect inversion of that old dream.

*　　*　　*

Vincom Mega Mall Smart City is surrounded by miles of flat rural land. Approaching at night, you drive through darkness for a while until a gilded village gradually appears, glittering with glass and LEDs. When the sun goes down, the checkpoints outside light up, and the community becomes gated. The skyscrapers, towering and sentient, are gridded with lights that flicker rhythmically and in coordination with the others, communicating in a language only they understand.

On my first morning in the unit, I look out the floor-to-ceiling window and find that the adjacent tower fills up the entire view. I can only see the sky from its reflection on the windows across from me. I press my weight against the cold glass windowpane to test its strength, gently then with force. Looking down, I can see slivers of street, pristine patches of lawn and vacant playgrounds, tiny like maquettes. It is eerily quiet, except for the distant sound of drilling, constant construction somewhere beyond the horizon.

To get a better view, I take the elevator to the pool lounge on the top floor. The turquoise tiles of the pool bounce light off a panoramic wall of windows, casting a cascade of reflections across the space. The lounge area seems like it has never been used. There are rows of plastic reclining chairs, an empty champagne bucket. I touch the water: frigid. I never see anyone here during my entire week-long stay.

Smart City feels designed for a class that has yet to fully emerge. In the meantime, it offers an aspirational model of living. The units vary in price, going up to over $1 million. The minimum wage in Vietnam is less than a dollar an hour.

While few citizens can afford to live here, the number of those who can afford to hoard this kind of real estate has been growing. Many of the units end up on AirBnB, where they are rented to people like me. Scrolling through the local listings, the options melt into perpetual déjà vu—specific yet indistinct, familiar yet formal, somewhere between a home and a hotel. Some seek to create personality with paintings and wall decals of inspirational quotes, but most are starkly minimal, devoid of any human pretense. All I see are bright laminate countertops, angular furniture with metal accents, pod homes for robots.

The social experience at Smart City is distinguished by the absence of long-term residents. When I pass other interlopers, we look at each other helplessly, like fish in neighboring bowls. No one is as alien as your neighbor, and a culture of transience increases the disconnect exponentially. What does this experience mean in a country like Vietnam, where millions of people died for socialist values and freedom from imperial hegemony only fifty years ago?

*   *   *

Like many enterprising businessmen of his generation, Vingroup founder Phạm Nhật Vượng studied in the Soviet Union during the late 1980s. In the course of the USSR's chaotic dissolution, he made what might have seemed an unwise move to Ukraine. Surrounded by a society collapsing in every meaningful sense, he started an instant noodle business, a cheap dietary solution for the lean conditions of the era. Phạm grew this enterprise into an empire of dehydrated culinary products, Technocom, which he would sell to Nestlé in 2009 for $150 million. Meanwhile, he began to reinvest in his home country, starting in 2003 with the construction of Vinpearl, a vacation resort in Nha Trang that has since exploded into an interlinking chain of services.

In recent years, journalists have warned that Vingroup's economic and political power has come to rival that of the government. The corporation has its own censorship apparatus, which it uses to sway coverage in its favor and scrub criticism from social media. One speck in a sprawling business universe, Vingroup's real estate arm almost seems like the benign part of the operation. Across the country, Vinhomes coexist with the relics of collective housing from the socialist period—at once underlining and belying the notion of continuity.

In Hanoi, Vinhomes sit alongside a type of mass housing complex unique to the city: the khu tập thể (KTT). Constructed under the North Vietnamese government in the late 1950s, these socialist collective housing units were the city's version of the Soviet microdistrict, a self-contained urban zone integrating various types of facilities. You can learn to spot the KTTs. Their architectural features blend inside and outside, both to provide relief from the tropical climate and to encourage a sense of communalism. Each unit is built not as an atomized living quarter but as part of a broader infrastructure and ecosystem. An outdoor corridor connects private living rooms and sleeping quarters to bathrooms and kitchens shared among families. "Tiger cages" on the windows create living extensions, concrete brise-soleil walls deflect sunlight and cast geometric patterns on the floor, and there are wide stairwells for ventilation, with short steps for children.

Standardized mass housing was one of the most important projects of state socialism. To live in a KTT was a point of pride and privilege. Now, the complexes are dilapidated and abandoned by the government, which has left upkeep to the aging inhabitants. Superficially, the Vinhomes appear as upgrades of the old model. To appreciate what was lost to this brutal transition, one needs to delve a little deeper into the history of the KTTs and consider their original purpose.

* * *

The first KTT I visit is one of a few built with wood drawn from a supply leftover by French-era construction. I am here with Trung Mai, an architect who trained and worked in Paris for over ten years before moving back to start Hà Nội Ad Hoc, an architecture firm with a thorough research-based praxis. He is working on a project cataloging the KTTs—marking their provenance, archiving them on a map.

Trung Mai's sentimentality toward socialist architecture feels uniquely diasporic, a disposition I recognize in myself. We come from subsequent waves of Việt kiều, a term used to designate Vietnamese returnees who have a reputation for taking a rosy-eyed view of the past. As we walk into the KTT, Trung Mai waves at the residents, who are washing dishes in the communal kitchen. "They know me," he says. "I'm always here."

I ask him if he is nostalgic.

"No!" he exclaims, surprising me with his sharp reaction. "I hate nostalgia. Everyone is nostalgic in this country. Everyone is always romanticizing the past. Haven't you noticed?"

That evening we meet architectural scholar Christina Schwenkel. Her book *Building Socialism* focuses on a unique KTT called Quang Trung in the town of Vinh. After the town was flattened by US aerial bombs, the Vietnamese Communist Party built these units with the help of the GDR in 1973, as a diplomatic gesture of red friendship.

Does the complex still exist? Parts of it have been demolished; neither Christina nor Trung Mai are sure how much of it remains. Trung Mai shows me a Facebook group called "*Thành Phố Vinh xinh đẹp*," which I read as "the city of Vinh so cute." There is a post and an accompanying photo set of Quang Trung from 2016. "As beautiful as the old movies," the post eulogizes, "the community areas are about to be dismantled."

I refuse to believe that it's all gone. Surely a few relics remain. Surely it left a lasting impression on its grounds.

The following night, I board a sleeper train and wake up the next morning in Vinh. The city is known as "the cradle of the Vietnamese revolution" because it's the proximate birthplace of the country's greatest nationalists, including poet Nguyễn Du and Hồ Chí Minh. The town's red tourist attractions include a visit to Hồ Chí Minh's house and the largest Hồ Chí Minh statue in the world, chiseled in a copper-colored granite that stands over fifty feet tall.

The town has long been depicted as a land of suffering, Schwenkel notes, where "harsh climate, bouts of warfare, persistent oppression, and natural catastrophes have produced a strong regional identity with distinctive cultural traits. The people are considered dauntless, hardworking, erudite, and rebellious, who live according to their own rule of law." Vinh's province, Nghệ An, was established as a political and industrial center under French rule. Our colonial overlords decided to merge three townships into one colonial municipality, creating the largest and poorest industrial city in Central Vietnam. A bad move, in retrospect: the same factories would launch the famous 1930s Nghệ-Tĩnh Soviets uprisings of Vietnamese peasants and intellectuals against the French regime, earning Vinh its proud nickname, Red City.

My friend Ngân, an interpreter who's accompanying me on the daytrip, tells me that the people in Vinh are notorious for their adaptive dialects. They are skilled at code-switching, throwing off their accents when applying for jobs because people are wary of hiring them. She says this as an ancient behemoth rises before us. Quang Trung is massive and sprawling, covering as much land as the Smart City complex. Much of it has been demolished. The few remaining buildings look singed by time. People still live here.

The 1972 US bombings halted Vinh's modernization, destroying critical infrastructure such as the inaugural train line, completed just months earlier. So it was with a certain defiance that the city chose, only two years after, to build one of the most ambitious housing projects in the country. On May 1, 1974, before a municipal crowd, the Minister of Construction laid the first bricks to rebuild Quang Trung, writes Schwenkel, "which included fragments from the wreckage of a downed US bomber—literally building imperial debris into the infrastructure of a future city."

Built to form ideal citizens and "new cultured families" based on a socialist modernist vision, the Quang Trung high-rises demonstrated the functionalist ideals of the rational city. They also enabled new forms of social regulation: the estate's unique design allowed authorities to surveil daily life more effectively.

The state designed Quang Trung in a way that facilitates air circulation and provides natural lighting. The buildings are spaced at a distance of at least one length of their height and arranged in a zigzag pattern. Quang Trung's plan is more human-centered than Smart City, which folds its inhabitants into compactly lined towers. It was centered around a small thoroughfare of cultural houses (*nhà văn hóa*) and leisure clubs common to socialist urban planning, which functioned as neighborhood community centers. The planners didn't consider leisure and recreation profitable activities or even part of the economic sector, but rather as rewards for deserving workers. The cultural house at Quang Trung remains in its original form and still runs free events but the movie theater has been demolished, replaced with a swanky commercial cineplex.

We can faintly detect the faded cement logo VD (Việt-Đức, or Vietnam-Germany), inscribed atop each entryway, as a secular talisman to ward off evil and bring luck to its inhabitants. When the complex was built, a rumor circulated that the buildings spell "Việt-Đức" when viewed from above.

Ngân and I sit in the courtyard leafing through Schwenkel's book, matching the historic photographs to the present surroundings. The central fountain no longer sprouts any water, and the playground is draped with clothing that appears to have been weathering rain for days. Quang Trung's disintegration began long ago; as with all the country's socialist complexes, construction stalled when the USSR dissolved. Though Quang Trung was envisioned as a utopian infrastructural project, a manifestation of socialist will, it has now became a symbol of state neglect. They have the look of what Schwenkel calls "unplanned obsolescence . . . the timelessness of socialist construction, its ability to transmit social and political values into the future through its material legacy, was 'timed out.'"

Often derided by mainstream news as the "least attractive" city in Vietnam, Vinh seems frozen in time. Its radical history has been preserved in small patches as a tourist attraction. The regional Nghệ An Museum exhibits blown out large-scale photographs of Quang Trung when it was first built in 1974, of Vietnamese women and German men clasping hands on top of the foundation bricks. Dusty vitrines display intricate socialist realist metal tableaux made from the scraps of downed US planes. In the parking lot, a group speaking in Korean depart a bus with a side panel that reads "let's go to the red address" ("đến với các địa chỉ đỏ"). On grounds where old socialist houses once stood, there are scaffolds for future towers, tightly clustered around each other. Out with the utopian, in with its futuristic opposite.

*   *   *

Driving back through the darkness toward Smart City, I feel darkly sentimental. *So this is what we have now instead*. The KTTs were also designed in self-sufficient zones that made space for all functions of life and work. They were built around communal services like kindergarten, shops, and medical care, and even provided staff housing for nearby state factories. Smart City recasts these rights as exalted privileges— private ventures rebranded as a commons. This is the corporate model of communal living, and it happens to track almost perfectly with the development of postwar Vietnam.

Urban planners are torn about what to do with the decaying KTT units throughout Hanoi. Should they be preserved as heritage sites in their original conditions, or should they be converted into hybrid models? Or demolished to make space for newer housing? Many of the units are in the center of the city, prime real estate, and are likely to be turned into high-density condominiums.

Back in Smart City, the towering example of late-capitalism as violent homogeneity, I find it ironic that socialist architecture was long described as brutal and monotonous. Whatever happened to capitalism's famous product: diversity?

Later that same night, the Wi-Fi in my unit goes out, right before an important Zoom call. Panicked,

I text the host. He gives me a key code and instructs me to go into a different unit, exactly three floors below mine, where there's reliable Wi-Fi. I take the elevator down to the thirty-first floor and enter an emptier version of my room—not a rental unit but more like a stopover home. An orange Louis Vuitton mohair jacket hangs on the coat rack. I open the refrigerator and behold its contents: thirty jars of bird's nest jelly. On the door shelves there's a card deck of luxury face masks. The writing on the package is Korean except for the ingredients: "progelina, horse placenta, dermcom, hyaluronic acid, collagen protein, salmon stem cells, cord blood stem cells."

I sit in the center of the empty room for my video call, my computer propped on the low glass table. A lamp on the floor lights my face from below. Among the Zoom windows, I am the only one in the dark. I find myself nodding off and am relieved when my colleagues decide to "break" a few minutes early. Packing up my computer, counting the steps from the door to the elevator and from there to my bed, my exhaustion starts to feel exquisite. Until I realize I am once again locked inside.

Culture Police

It's an hour before an opening reception at Sàn Art, an independent gallery space in Ho Chi Minh City, when two officers walk in. They've arrived to review the new exhibition—nine pieces of neon art.

Curator Nhật Q Võ darts up from where we're all sitting and greets the two visitors with practiced hospitality. Võ and his colleagues have secured a license for the show, submitting artist bios and detailed explanations of every work to the Ministry of Culture, Sports, and Tourism. The officers are here to verify that everything matches the application.

We look on with frozen grins as Võ guides the two men around the loft space. The neon pieces haven't been plugged in yet, rendering them unintelligible—empty marquees full of glass tubing—leaving Võ free to elaborate. *Neon captures the spirit of the modern metropolis*, he expounds, *its electric dreams and nocturnal poetry*. This is a common strategy for dealing with the culture police: disarm them with pleasantries, then overwhelm them with abstract concepts until their eyes glaze over. Dwell on grandiose themes, nothing too pointed, until they're itching to move on with their day. The officers are there to tick items off their list, after all, not entertain the philosophy of art.

The efficacy of this approach varies from officer to officer. Are they feeling motivated that day? Well-rested? Hungry? This undue authority makes them a natural subject for derision. A folk poem summarizes the qualifications required for landing a job at state agencies, in order of importance: nepo baby, connections, money, intelligence (*"thứ nhất hậu duệ, thứ nhì quan hệ, thứ ba tiền tệ, thứ tư trí tuệ."*)

The rest of us murmur amongst ourselves in English, a language many officers don't speak. Our chatter skips a beat as Võ leads them past one of the dicier pieces. A neon sign by Dinh Q Lê reads "Monumental! Long Live!" (*"Vĩ Đại! Muôn Năm!"*), a slogan typically adorning socialist realist billboards. The rococo frame in which it is enclosed—ornate, and wrapped in silver leaf—refers to a decadent style popular among the wealthy political class, who move freely between big business and big government. Võ sidesteps this subtext and instead portrays the work as an homage to the nation's resilient spirit.

This kind of obfuscation has deep enough roots in Vietnam to merit its own idiom: *"nghĩa bóng nghĩa đen,"* which directly translates to "shiny meaning black meaning." The phrase evokes a translucent sphere that's so reflective you can't see what's going on inside. This tradition of wordplay, the centuries-old penchant for aphorism, comes in handy when dealing with the state's censorship apparatus.

The officers seem at once bored and satisfied with Võ's explanations but demand the gallery refile one of their forms. Pleased to have done something, they go on their merry way. "Lackeys," a curator mutters as the door closes. "Fools."

Once the coast is clear, Sàn Art feels like an international contemporary art space again. The censorship regime is only discernible in the subtlety of the work on display; and in the marked differences between

the handouts printed in English and Vietnamese.
The English descriptions flaunt the subversive intent
of the work, while the Vietnamese text offers a master-
class in "shiny meaning black meaning."

*   *   *

Artists helped build the Communist republic. In the
early years following the August Revolution of 1945,
the Việt Minh conscripted painters, poets, novelists,
and playwrights to develop the country's cultural
and media organizations. In the early years, their
mission was clear: promote socialism, reunification with
the South, and vigilance against imperial aggression—
but make it beautiful. This message needed to reach
people across class divides and literacy levels; hence
the turn toward socialist realism.

As the Party formalized its cultural policies,
elevating one form of art to the forced exclusion
of all others, some of these same artists started to feel
like useful idiots. By the 1950s, they had mounted
a movement for cultural freedom known as the
Nhân Văn–Giai Phẩm affair; like many forms of
dissent, it would be squashed by military violence and
specialized re-education camps. This confrontation
exposed such fundamental divisions that the Southern
government repurposed the protest materials for
their own anti-communist campaigns. Following
reunification in 1975, the North extended its policies
South, establishing an Arts Association to ensure
compliance of all cultural production with its guidelines. Formerly regime-friendly artists from the

South were rounded up, brutalized, and sent to "self-criticism school."

Today's Ministry of Culture has inherited the Ministry of Propaganda's practices, but none of its purpose. Its predecessor organization had a clear mandate: "to raise political consciousness, patriotism, love of labor, love of class, the collective spirit, the internationalist spirit," and to "construct national culture, make good use of past heritage, combine with the fight against enslaving culture, and eradicate vestiges of the enemy's culture." Such directives made strategic sense for a nation under imperial attack, building toward a communist utopia. Today, these totalitarian control mechanisms feel like vestigial organs. They raise an obvious but nonetheless unspoken question: why are we still doing this?

What exactly is prohibited now? According to Clause 8 of the Decree 23/2019/ND-CP for Exhibition Activities, one can't show anything that "advocates against the government, instigates war and conflict among ethnicities, falsifies historical facts, discloses an organization's secret without having its consent, or violates civilized lifestyles." The vagueness is the point. It's hard to know what counts as "falsifying historical facts" in a country that consistently rewrites its own history.

In her ambitious survey "Artistic Freedom Report Vietnam: An Ever-changing Terrain," Saigon-based curator Linh Lê tries to list all the artworks taken down between 2010 and 2022, counting a total of eighty-one. Most often, the stated reason was "violation of original traditions and fine customs" ("*vi phạm thuần phong mỹ tục*"). Annoyingly, Lê writes, "no one knows what these traditions and customs are."

Sometimes the reasons for punishment are hard to discern. Lê raises the case of Bùi Chát, who won the International Freedom to Publish Prize in 2011 for cultural organizing, only to be detained upon returning to Vietnam. The authorities banned his books, forcing him to become a private citizen, and when he finally resurfaced a decade later with a show of abstract paintings, they doubled down. The People's Committee not only fined him for exhibiting without a license but scheduled all his works to be destroyed. Though these charges were retracted due to widespread press coverage and criticism on social media, the Party had once again made its point.

It's hard to know if you're breaking the rules because they change constantly. When Vietnam's territorial disputes with the People's Republic of China over the South China Sea intensified in 2016, authorities began banning all media featuring maps with the "nine-dash line," a demarcation the PRC uses to claim rights over the body of water. In the lead-up to this year's fiftieth anniversary of Reunification, the government began to normalize relations with the US by tamping down on criticism of American imperialism— an ironic turn, to put it mildly.

To the public, this imperfect state of affairs represents progress. Today's censorship apparatus seems lenient compared to previous enforcement regimes, not to mention current practices in neighboring countries like China. Nonetheless, Vietnam still ranks among the globe's worst free speech offenders according to the World Press Freedom Index, routinely imprisoning activists, religious leaders, union organizers, journalists, and academics for dissidence.

The state's regulation of the art world, meanwhile, stands out for its inconsistency. Direct interventions, such as exhibition shutdowns, equipment confiscation, and arrests are infrequent, but still occur regularly enough to maintain a culture of fear and paranoia. This arrangement has an odd side effect: forcing functionaries to think like artists, and artists to think like functionaries.

✳   ✳   ✳

"The social role of the artist in Vietnamese society is rather confused," curator and former Sàn Art artistic director Zoe Butt writes in a 2014 essay. Many would rather make introspective works than demand "the right to freedom of speech and civil liberties."

Even overtly political works leave room for plausible deniability. One powerful example of this, Butt and Dinh Q Lê raise in a talk, is Tuan Andrew Nguyen's 2009 sculpture *Enemy's Enemy: A Monument to a Monument*—a baseball bat engraved with the iconic image of Buddhist monk Thích Quảng Đức's self-immolation in 1963. On closer inspection, the carving doesn't depict the monk's famous act of protest, but a monument the government erected in his honor. Considering the regime's historic repression of Buddhism, the work becomes a commentary on how the state appropriates historical events to serve its own narrative. This critique, of course, is only expressed plainly in English descriptions of the work. These are the symbolic games one must play to make a statement.

Artists have become masters of double speak—conveying meaning while technically saying nothing at all. "The most important thing for Vietnamese visual artists is to know where to push and where to hold back," an anonymous source tells scholar Samantha Libby. "Sneaking is an important skill . . . Many of us create artwork with multiple layers of meaning so we can explain it to different audiences. It is a dangerous but also exciting game." The maneuvers become part of the craft.

The dance between artists and authorities has only become more elaborate since Vietnam liberalized its economy and opened markets to foreign investment in 1987. One reason for this has been the rise of MFA-style art practices, which have proven to be as inscrutable to the state as they are to most people. Sàn Art, founded in 2007 by a group of artists with US degrees, have done pioneering work in this regard. While established art schools continued teaching portraiture and lacquer painting, Sàn Art came to function as a modern para-academic space, offering residencies, philosophy seminars, and studio critiques where discourse was as important as the art itself. Art, in this new context, was not about mastery or even objects, but ideas.

"Sàn Art Laboratory gave us license to experiment," artist Trương Công Tùng reflects in a catalog essay. While their approach may have set out to challenge conventional art education and prepare artists for the international market, it simultaneously offered a practical local strategy.

In anticipation of an unusually direct 2010 exhibition at Sàn Art—the artist Nguyễn Thái Tuấn's *Fullness of Absence*—the curators turned to interpretation as preemptive protection from censorship. The series of paintings depicts invisible figures in modern business attire set within the palace of Vietnam's last Emperor, Bảo Đại—a backdrop that invites parallels between today's wealthy "Communist" elite and the monarch ousted by the Việt Minh. In one painting, an olive-green police uniform hovers over a set of civilian clothes, the officer's sleeve raised, ready to strike.

The curators drafted four different press releases: one for the government, two for local press, and one for international audiences. Still, the Ministry prohibited some works, according to Butt, insisting there should only be "either paintings illustrating pre-1975 or post-1975 and not together." This directive seemed arbitrary but was in fact incredibly pointed. Sàn Art responded by placing the sanctioned paintings in a backroom, which became a speakeasy-style extension of the show.

The internet offered little refuge. When Sàn Art published Nguyễn's statement online, comparing colonial rulers to today's new elites, the Ministry ordered them to take it down. The revised statement reads: "Fully clothed men and women with no bodies sit within seemingly anonymous spaces akin to a hotel room, where the direction of light creates particular shadows on the floors and walls . . . Hats, coats, and shoes are sentimentally painted, like a kind of memory that has been carefully nurtured." You can choose whether or not to hear the sardonic undertone.

*   *   *

In authoritarian countries with limited independent cultural spaces, contemporary art experiences a double reception—one in its immediate context and one in the globalized art world, where freer circulation might be achieved. While using art to channel otherwise forbidden information and criticism is a hopeful idea, one that I personally remain invested in, it also begs difficult questions about access and audience. Relying on the opaque language of contemporary art creates a gap between what local audiences can perceive and what international viewers can interpret. This set-up turns curators into intermediaries between the Vietnamese state and the international art market, tasked with lubricating any frictions.

None of this is to diminish what artists and curators have managed to do in these conditions, but to point out that many of the works that float under the state's radar also fly over most people's heads. These are, in the end, concessions to power.

In their original cultural policies, the state expressed open contempt for intellectuals, rejecting what it considered elitist art in favor of accessibility. Decades later, this same state has created a situation where artists must envelop their perspectives in layers of formal and theoretical complexity just to survive. Artistic expression, like its institutions, has been privatized. Yesterday's public cultural houses and theaters have been replaced by private art galleries and art spaces in high-rise condos. Sàn Art, for instance, is in a residential loft. All visits are intentional. There is no "stumbling in."

When a censorship regime reaches a certain age, it inevitably comes full circle and starts censoring its old output. This absurdity reaches new heights when bureaucrats are confronted with state-funded historical materials. I have witnessed this while curating exhibitions from a private collection of propaganda art. For one show, we included a set of double-sided posters that present a striking contrast: one side of the posters featured soft sketches of people in positions of repose, made during a figure-drawing class. Years later, when the Party turned its directives toward fighting imperialism, artists facing paper shortages repurposed these sketches, drawing agitprop for the war effort on the reverse.

Officials who reviewed our license application flagged these posters, objecting to the nudity of the figure drawings and to the fact that there were drawings on both sides. It's a vivid example of being beholden to an evaluation system that doesn't know its own history. Creating art is hard enough; it is maddening to do it at the whim of people who only know how to destroy it.

My North Vietnamese Friend

I

I saw X sitting at the end of the bar and walked over so
eagerly that I almost barged into him. It was our second
near-collision of the day. That morning, we had run
into each other on the street. He, an acquaintance from
my previous visit to Hanoi, turned out to be living
around the corner from me. I hadn't slept that night
and so it all felt like a great coincidence. This, I should
have known, was the humbling panic of the incipient
crush, when someone so alien abruptly feels familiar.

I had come to Hanoi on a research grant to
study the Vietnamese independence movement and
its culture, a self-appointed mission that at times felt
like my calling, and others like a misguided exercise
in diasporic yearning. X is the same age as me and
so had experienced the life I had forsaken when my
parents and I immigrated to the US from Saigon.
He was amused by my suburban American upbringing
but didn't envy it. Born and raised in Hanoi, he was
confident in his history.

The bar was close to the train tracks that run
through the Old Quarter. People drink and socialize
on the tracks, stumbling off the path when a train
arrives, its horn roaring. Sitting against a wall, we
watched tourists pose for photos, angling their bodies
only feet from the hurtling machines. Rows of rice
wine infusions lined the bar's shelves, along with glass
bottles stuffed with herbs and garlic cloves, coiled
snakes and animal intestines.

We ordered a bottle of honeycomb wine and caught each other up on all that had happened in the seven years since we'd last seen each other. He told me about his life in the city, and maybe it was the liquor, but a sadness started to seep through my body. Was this lust or envy? He knew the depths of Hanoi in a way that no amount of study could ever replicate. I steadied myself by gazing at the tiny, gold flecks floating in our honeycomb wine. They looked familiar. Where had I seen those flecks before?

We left the bar wasted and walked along the train tracks. The night air was frigid and smelled of gasoline. We stumbled through a stretch of fog until we made out the Temple of Literature in the distance. Surrendering to the story of the night, we decided to hop the fence. The sprawling campus was built in 1070 on the ground of Vietnam's first university to honor the sacred pursuit of study. There are lines of stelae, or stone slabs, inscribed with the names and achievements of scholars who passed imperial examinations. Some of the stelae balance atop turtle statues. I had been coming to the temple in the mornings to study the turtles. Now he was there with me.

We walked by the gnarled trees that have been growing there for centuries. We arrived at the pond Thiên Quang, or "Heaven Light," in the middle of the courtyard, which was designed to mirror the sky, reflecting the twin kingdoms of heaven and scholarship. Maybe we kissed, but that doesn't matter.

I woke up in the evening the next day feeling impossibly clearheaded. I responded to messages I had

been ignoring for weeks. Cascading gold flecks—
I suddenly remembered. In a previous research phase,
I had read about Christians in the Middle Ages
who reported seeing gold flecks descend from the sky
during ecstatic visions. An impossible image that I
could now faintly imagine. I felt an urgency to tell X.
I wanted to tell X everything.

II

Optimism is erotic. In an image from the pages of
Vietnam Pictorial (*Hình Ảnh Việt-Nam*)—one of the
Communist Party's longest-running magazines,
launched five months after the Việt Minh defeated
the French troops in 1954—a boy and a girl are envel-
oped by a field of flowers. The photo collage is from
1957: soft reds, pinks, and whites, a blossoming
hill under an open sky. The flowers are the size of
the children's faces. It's a mild type of dramatization,
fantasy unto the imaginable.

Factories of glowing chrome machines, women
in pristine lab coats, gleaming metals of industry
and collectivization. These images, scholar Thy Phu
writes in *Warring Visions*, are better understood
as "photographic paintings." Aligning the "realism
of photography with the fantastical contrivances of
propaganda posters," the hand-treated color "lent
definition and vibrancy to a reality that appeared
rooted in the present yet was still to come." This subtle
enhancement encapsulates the fantasy-within-reach
appeal of socialist realism—shock for the idealist,
pleasure for the materialist.

These were the types of things I had come to
Hanoi to study: the paintings, posters, films, and
photographs classified as propaganda or wartime art,
an ecosystem of romantic optimism rendered across
media. I was drawn to a broad and somewhat arbitrary
window, between 1945 and 1975—after the August

Revolution and the Việt Minh's victory over the French, before the Fall of Saigon. I imagined this period as an existential triumph, a cleavage in time when anything seemed possible—an outbreak of love before things hardened into rule.

Historians agree that the Communists prevailed in 1945, among the many anticolonial forces, because they were the most organized. Less often acknowledged, however, is the creativity of the enterprise—their robust art and culture strategy. The Việt Minh and the Communist Party's intellectual affiliates considered art and literature essential tools in the struggle for national independence, unification, and socialist revolution. In this realm, too, centralization required consensus. This was hard to come by. It would take a decade before the regime rolled out the Democratic Republic of Vietnam's official culture policy, overseen by General Secretary of Culture Trường Chinh. Going forward, artists and writers would be conscripted to make realist literature and art—so crucial to the Soviet and Chinese revolutions. Nguyễn Thị Định, Party leader and one of the chief authors of the cultural guidelines, touted realism as a way to "establish models of the social life that is growing" and to "make tomorrow appear in the midst of today." This was Marxist-Leninism at its most exalted.

Today, socialist realism is deemed a niche subject, which is ironic, because it was intended to captivate the hearts and minds of all people. The popularity of the aesthetic style is still evident on billboards through-out Vietnam: old posters stand out against more recent state billboards, which offer crude, generic remixes of the old vision. They both celebrate archetypes: simple cartoons of nurses, doctors, agriculturalists, engineers; men, women, and children, all playing their parts; vocations deemed necessary for the advancement of socialist society. People may still be fascinated by these posters as kitsch, but no one is taken by their spectral power.

I've learned over the years that my fascination with propaganda art is not necessarily shared by friends who live in Vietnam. To me, what stands out is the promise of the revolution—what could have been and still could be. If I had spent my whole life here, the broken promises that followed would probably be more resonant.

How did my interest in this aesthetic world begin? I certainly didn't grow up with it in America. Maybe that's the reason why it gripped me, because I wasn't supposed to like it. I remember in college when my grandmother saw my books and expressed concern that I was in possession of Marxist texts. "Won't you get in trouble for carrying those?" No, I told her. Repression doesn't quite work that way here.

Vietnam Pictorial's outlook was future-facing. Given that emphasis, Phu observes, it may seem strange that some of the hand-colored images don't depict technological prowess but idyllic, agrarian scenes. The photographs are "awash in the sentimental flush of timeliness [and point] nostalgically to a past far removed from the metallic radiance of a triumphal future to come." This sense of religious steadfastness was a mainstay of Vietnamese Communism, which combined Marxism and Confucianism through "the continuity thesis." Influenced by Ludwig Feuerbach's *The Essence of Christianity*, Marx proffered love as the highest state of humanity. "The essence internal to all human relations is love," Marx wrote in his "Theses on Feuerbach." "Men's political, economic, and ideological conflicts are the quarrels of lovers who know not that they love." Marx's faith is defined by a state of waiting, an almost religious conviction that communism will arrive.

In certain religious texts, the tenses that distinguish past, present, and future become interchangeable. Old Testament theology, for instance, is written in what is called the prophetic present tense, where a present perfect, or past perfect tense may be used to refer to the future. There is a similar predictive affirmation in socialist realist rhetoric. The Việt Minh would write speeches to the masses using anticipatory verbs, describing plans as if they had already happened.

III

Falling in love is, among other things, the quickest form of information exchange. X and I would message each other throughout the day, usually while I was surrounded by a dusty moat of catalogs at the Vietnam Film Institute. I was reading about the Vietnam Film School, the first of its kind. When Hồ Chí Minh established the Vietnam Movie and Photography Enterprise in 1953, he articulated a two-part task for national cinema: "to build socialism, and to struggle for the liberation of the South for the reunification of the country." Vietnamese cinema became established during extreme political and economic instability, and, later, genocidal carpet-bombing. Guerillas set up film development labs in war zones, sourcing their equipment from solidarity groups around the world.

In 1959, the Vietnam Film School opened its doors. The Party handled its distribution, taking screenings across Vietnam and the Red world. That year, the Film Unit produced the country's first narrative feature film, *On the Same River* (*Chung Một Dòng Sông*) by Nguyễn Hồng Nghi and Phạm Kỳ Nam, which retold the story of revolution from the perspective of the peasantry. The film centers on two lovers separated by a river at the seventeenth parallel, a line drawn through the country and enforced by the US military after the 1954 Geneva Conference. Hoài, a young woman from the South, and Vận, a fisherman from the

North, are separated at the beginning and reunited at the end. The personification of national interests through lovers would endure in national cinema for decades, even in Đặng Nhật Minh's 1984 *When the Tenth Month Comes* (*Bao giờ cho đến tháng Mười*), the first Vietnamese film shown in the US.

The state archives mainly contain records from the North, though anticolonial and anti-imperial dissent was burgeoning everywhere. The Việt Minh were not the only, or even the first, group to make revolutionary cinema. Communist filmmakers from the South had created a type of film called Bưng Biền–Đồng Tháp Mười in the 1940s. A civilian who witnessed Bưng Biền described it "the crystallization of romance from people who dare to think and dare to do." This activity was squashed, and the Southern communists were erased from history.

I texted X a photo of the roster from Vietnam Film School's first class. "What if instead of academic research I wrote an erotic screenplay about the film school?"

"It would certainly be more fun to read."

"A Southern schoolgirl has just left dance class and kneels by the courtyard fountain to lace one of her slippers. She hears a voice from above her, a crisp, zippy accent. She looks up to see her classmate, a Northern boy, haloed by the sunlight, hair swept across his face. Smirking down at her, he extends his hand. 'Did you hear?' He asks. 'The school is starting a cinematography class.' He pulls her upright and lightly holds her by the waist for balance as they face each other. He looks into her eyes: 'Should we make a movie together?'"

"Do they fuck?" X asked.

"Yes, but this is a Vietnamese film, so we don't see it."

He told me about *The Sorrow of War* (*Nỗi buồn chiến tranh*), a 1991 novel based on the author Bảo Ninh's time as a North Vietnamese soldier. Bảo was one of the five hundred soldiers who went to war in 1969 with the Glorious 27th Youth Brigade and one of ten to survive.

The story is narrated by a middle-aged soldier named Kien, who is tasked with collecting the bodies of his comrades from the jungles of Central Vietnam. Waiting for a bombing run to cease, Kien recalls seeing friends scorched by napalm or dying slow deaths due to malnutrition. He also recounts the salacious details of the women he slept with and fantasies of others he encountered. Though Bảo denies any relation to the protagonist, the novel is clearly autobiographical.

"It's a crushing story of disillusionment," X said to me. "It's one horny book."

"Revolutionary romance," or *lãng mạn cách mạng*, was the Party's designated aesthetic form. The Việt Minh were influenced by Soviet philosophy and Mao's notion of the "contradictory unity" of realism and romanticism, but also looked to their own country's dramatic literary tradition. Leaders like Hồ Chí Minh, Trường Chinh, and Tố Hữu presented themselves as poets and filled Party recruitment materials with sentimental rhetoric. They drew on the works of past literary movements like New Poetry (*Thơ Mới*) and rewrote them. "Feelings and Emotion," penned in 1938 by one of New Poetry's biggest stars, Xuân Diệu, was adjusted so that the dreams of clouds and winds in the original were replaced by dreams of destroying the brute forces of imperialism. This method was highly effective and persuaded many intellectuals to join the Party. As the poet Nguyễn Tuân remarked, "It changed my view away from art for art's sake toward life."

Politicizing love forces difficult questions. How does the notion of revolutionary love relate to the romantic love one feels for a person? Is the couple a formal hindrance to societal love, as Herbert Marcuse argues in *Eros and Civilization*, or can the two coexist? Is the goal of love under communism to subordinate individual romance to love for the collective? As the philosopher Christian Lotz writes, "love is a form of being social in which the sensual life is as complex as the social world, and not simply an abstraction from the latter."

That is to say: the more you love, the more you exist. Your capacity to learn expands, your sensitivities are heightened. Your audience is defined, your stakes are clarified. Love makes a different life feel possible. In this way, the two senses of romance do not appear so different at all.

IV

One afternoon X and I visited Thanh Uy, a gallery of graphic art a few miles outside central Hanoi. It belongs to an herbal medication magnate who has spent his career amassing historic lithographs and etchings, woodcuts and engravings, screenprints and paintings, learning the intricate details of every piece. We stood in front of a 1971 etching titled *Revenge* (*Trả Thù*) by the artist Lê Huy Tiếp. A man without a shirt or shoes walks past a scatter of skulls and bones. There is a certain vitality in his stride. He wields a knife. Three floating beings surround him—ghosts of the martyred. The ghosts' faces are contorted in anguish. One of them has her hand pressed gently on his back as they guide him, pointing the way. Together they move toward a radiant sun that is dripping with something viscous like blood.

I was surprised by the work's incandescent grief, its contrast to the stoic expressions in most socialist art. Lê made this etching when the US was in its seventh year of an annihilationist bombing campaign. The "US air war" decade would decimate whole family trees and flatten entire towns to rubble. Such a severe campaign could only be justified if the people on the ground were not perceived as fully human. The US military didn't count human casualties as dutifully as they counted destroyed trucks, trees, bridges, tunnels, and smokestacks.

The invocation of emotion in Vietnamese propaganda, then, might be considered an act of *rehumanization*: a reclamation of a common humanity, for themselves and an international audience. Love becomes one expression alongside anger and anguish in a spectrum of propulsive emotions. It is harder to fathom killing people who love each other.

At the Vietnam Film Institute, I watched another masterpiece of emotion-as-strategy, the 1974 film *The Little Girl of Hanoi* (*Em bé Hà Nội*), directed by Hải Ninh, who graduated from one of the first cohorts of the Vietnam Film School's directing class. It was made in reaction to the "Christmas bombings" of December 1972, during which at least ten thousand tons of explosives were dropped, mainly on Hanoi. By the end of the twelve-day assault, an estimated sixteen thousand Vietnamese people had been killed. For the film, Hải drew on civilian accounts of the bombardments. Hải himself hid in a wet, cold, fully packed shelter with his daughter.

Set in Khâm Thiên, the most severely bombed area in Hanoi, the film is narrated by an eleven-year-old girl named Ngọc Hà who is looking for her father. She meets a soldier during her search, and their conversations cut to sequences of her memories. The film opens with a bus, full of children, coasting along a road. A girl's ebullient voice sings: *I walk across city streets, filled with love*. The film is remarkable not only for its privileging of the perspective of a child, but for how this perspective departs from militant cinema's standard convention of emphasizing the nation's fighting spirit. The viewer sees the world and the ravages of destruction, as well as love and intimacy, through the eyes of a noncombatant. *Little Girl* is filled with affection. Ngọc Hà holds her teddy bear and is held in turn by her mother and grandmother. In a scene in which she surveys the wreckage of her house, she weeps among stoic adults. By "mapping tenderness onto the inexpressibility of pain and the rubble that the war causes," the scholar Qui-Ha Hoang Nguyen writes, *Little Girl* presents a vision "of the agency of the damaged."

The following day, I came home to my apartment to a package wrapped in a brown paper bag leaning against the door. Inside was Bảo Ninh's *The Sorrow of War*. I brought the book to the couch. From the window, I had a direct view of the high-rise tower where X worked—where, in fact, he was at that very moment. Maybe he could see me.

Bảo Ninh recalls that when he joined the Party at the age of seventeen, he was swept up by the songs and literature at recruitment camps. When the war ended, the government hailed him and other surviving soldiers as victors. But he didn't feel heroic. He felt broken. *The Sorrow of War* was his final project at Hanoi's Nguyễn Du Writing School, established after the war to train writers to support the new state. It took him a decade to muster the courage to put the story on paper.

His friends collected money to print copies of the book. *The Sorrow of War* circulated underground, among students, because its candid reflections bristled against the official state narrative. But Bảo Ninh was writing precisely for the soldiers who were uncritically exalted by the Party, whose tortured lives deserved honest assessment.

"No one could read those kinds of [state-produced] novels," he said. "How could you stand a book that praised you to stupidity?" The Party banned *The Sorrow of War* when it was published.

X was right. The novel is as sensuous as it is abject. Kien's narration happens at the precipice of death, in a fugue state where dreams are indistinguishable from memories. His descriptions glitter with sentiment, as if he were recalling mystical lands rather than warscapes:

> I was back standing in the Jungle of Screaming Souls. The stream, the dirt road, the empty grass clearings, the edge of the forest of days gone by, were sparkling in sunshine. I was standing in this peaceful, picturesque scene, looking Southwest towards the four olive green peaks of Ngoc Bo Ray mountain, when my new dream adventure began.

Kien's reflections on love bring him psychological and physical relief from his destitution, affirming a life well-lived. He thinks back to the time "before the cruelty and destruction of war had warped his soul," when "he had been aching with desire, hilarious, frivolous, and lighthearted," when "he was worthy of being a lover and in love." In moments when Kien's condition seems especially dire, his reminiscences become religious. He describes gazing at the sky and seeing a "heavenly glow," which "streaked, sparkled, and vanished like a falling star" and, for a fleeting moment, "bathed him in serene light."

Though Bảo Ninh himself disavowed the Party's glorified narrative, Kien's reflections on his role as a soldier dovetail with the holy steadfastness of socialist realism: "In contemplation an odd idea takes root in his mind . . . At the bottom of his heart he believes he exists on this earth to perform some unnamed heavenly duty." The first time Kien feels this "sacred force" is while he is on an assignment in the jungles to gather the remains of the dead:

> The force nurtured him, protected him, and willed him on, renewing his thirst for living and for love. He had never before acknowledged this heavenly duty, yet he had always known it existed within him as an integral part of him, melded with his soul.

Like *Little Girl*, Bảo Ninh's novel gives agency to the damaged. Though *The Sorrow of War* became an international bestseller when it was translated into English in 1994, the author struggled to convince Vietnamese authorities to lift the local ban. "He never understood why his book was banned by the government, you know," the poet Nguyễn Quang Thiều remarked. "He was just sad about what happened. And he wrote about it."

In the years following the August Revolution, everything seemed to be in flux. The shared goal of liberation and the agency of the artist did not yet seem mutually exclusive. They could even be symbiotic. But there were limits: after the end of French colonial rule, Western art and literature were generally derided, as individualistic, bourgeois, and counter-revolutionary.

The Marxist scholar and critic Đặng Thai Mai, who received a Franco-Vietnamese education at the College of Pedagogy in Hanoi in the 1920s, belonged to a transitional generation that reevaluated the colonial influence on their education. Appointed to the Cultural Association for National Salvation to draft guidelines for art and literature under socialism, Đặng renounced his past. In a series of articles spanning the late 1940s, he made a passionate argument against art for art's sake, stressing the social responsibility of the artist in an age of revolutionary struggle. Only when a piece has broad social relevance does it become art:

> While a world, a regime, is still disintegrating, if
> we recognize that neutrality is only a meaningless
> term and that the freedom of an individual
> cannot be disconnected from public life and that
> the meaning of art can only be realized within
> the community, within human society, then
> we also must realize that the new art and literature
> must flower in social reality, and it must be
> art and literature of the "socialist-realist" kind.

These broadsides set off a vehement public debate about whether art and propaganda were interchangeable. What distinguished one from the other? In those years, propaganda (*tuyên truyền*) did not have a negative connotation, and many Party leaders proclaimed that it was indeed exchangeable with art. Propaganda is persuasion, and art, at its most effective, is persuasive. "Literature and art are a kind of propaganda without propagandizing," Cultural Association leader Nguyễn Đình Thi argued, "and precisely because of this they are the most effective form of propaganda."

Both Đặng and Nguyễn's lines of argument elicited mixed reactions and prompted a public rebuke by the outspoken and well-respected painter Tô Ngọc Vân. One of the first graduates of the Indochinese College of Fine Arts, Tô was a prominent painter known for his classical paintings of high-society women and an ardent defender of beauty. "Art has changed our way of life," he stated. It "made everyone aware of beauty in a more understanding manner."

Expressing his concern in a 1947 article titled "Propaganda and Art," Tô wrote that "propaganda art is not true art because it expresses a political purpose, raises political slogans, delineates a political path for the people to follow, and displays situations that will generate in them a political attitude." Art, on the other hand, "was an expression of an individual soul, an attitude of an individual toward things, telling his feelings more than philosophy about any issue."

He built to a bold conclusion: "Art has everlasting value while propaganda art has only temporary value." It was one thing for the Party to decide to prioritize propaganda production over art during a crisis ("in our people's period of struggle today, this temporary value is bigger than the eternal value of the artistic treasures of mankind"); it was a grave error to conflate the two.

Doubling down in a letter to Tô the following year, Đặng asserted that an artist was invariably a propagandist for one ideology or another and that the work was only of value when it supported a "progressive" goal. Tô shot back: "It is erroneous to conclude that propaganda art could approach the level of true art!" Art and propaganda art, he emphasized, used different techniques to reach different goals. It is as absurd to demand that all art be persuasive in a literal sense as it is to insist propaganda be subtle and unique as art; it is an "illogical invasion injurious to the art of propaganda, which by its nature must be plain and clear." To conflate them was a disservice to *both*.

This exchange would become known as the Tô Ngọc Vân-Đặng Thai Mai debates. The General Secretary of Culture Trường Chinh addressed both positions but ultimately affirmed Đặng's orthodox view:

> When propaganda achieves a certain level, it becomes art. When art reaches a particular level of effectiveness, art clearly has a propagandistic nature. Thus, there may exist propagandists who are not or not yet artists, but it cannot be that there are artists who are not propagandists entirely.

Trường's view would become official policy. In 1949, the Party established more restrictive guidelines. Tô was reined in and privately remained torn between his two identities—the nationalist and the artist. "Here lies the principal point, the torment of my soul," he wrote in the newspaper *Văn Nghệ* in 1949, "how to make the self that serves the nation and the masses and the self that serves art—the artist of course cannot forget this responsibility—not to come into conflict or, even worse, betray one another."

V

On my first visit to Hanoi in 2017, my aunt took me on a tour. We visited the mausoleum where Hồ Chí Minh's body is on display, though there is some speculation as to whether the body is truly his. The state history tour was a spectacle of memorialization, all pomp and circumstance. The whole process can take a few hours. In a group of twenty or so, we observed a choreographed dance, then were brought into a theater to watch films about the Party's valiant efforts to liberate the country.

During one of the films—newsreel footage of Hồ Chí Minh's funeral and the procession that led up to viewing his recently deceased body—my aunt started to cry. She dabbed her cheek with a handkerchief. What was she feeling? Did the scene genuinely move her, or was this reaction ingrained, a response to some kind of cue? Is there a difference? After the footage ended, we were ushered in a steady line to see the famous corpse. The room was dimly lit, and the line moved quickly. I tried to take as much time as I could. I craned my neck to look at the supine figure, squinting to see if it was really him. The guards nudged us along. Why did the Communists have such a strong penchant for embalming the body?

For me, my family has always personified the notion of domestic love as a small island of communism —how love can activate a radically non-transactional way of relating. My aunt and my uncle, two of six siblings in my mom's family, never married. They are in their fifties and sixties and live with my grandmother in the same house where they were born and raised, where I was born and raised, in Saigon. They care for my grandmother every day, cooking for her, washing her clothing by hand, bathing her, assisting her every trip to the bathroom.

When my grandmother wakes up, my aunt gazes at her and asks, "How is my precious jewel? How is the love of my life?" It is the most rarefied devotion, to commit to taking care of someone for the rest of their days.

About ten years ago, my uncle bought a farmhouse in Củ Chi, a rural area an hour outside of Saigon's city center. The farmhouse is near the site of the famous Củ Chi tunnels, part of an extensive underground network created by the Việt Cộng, which they used during the 1968 Tết Offensive. National history can be bittersweet in the South; for my family it is both a source of collective pride and a reminder of violent destitution. Like Hồ Chí Minh's mausoleum park, the entire area around the tunnels has been revamped into a tourist attraction.

Last year, my uncle, aunt, grandmother, and I visited the park to see artifacts of Vietnamese victory. During our visit, a dented US UH-1A helicopter was displayed on the lawn. The placard read "one of hundreds of aircraft shot down and captured by the liberation guerillas of the South." Nearby, there was an exhibition of explosives, cluster bombs, and rocket launchers, collected from around the area. The weapons were assembled in neat rows under straw roofs. The metal plates affixed to the sides of the bombs revealed their provenance: "Dispenser Aircraft SUU-30B/B, Camden, USA." To this day there are still undetonated bombs all over Vietnam, which all-women volunteer groups locate and dig up with their bare hands. We were taken into an auditorium where an animated video about underground guerillas was playing. It included depictions of their living quarters and elaborate defense tactics, set to bombastic electronic music.

Many red tourist attractions feature frontline fighters in wax, smiling modestly in their original uniforms. At the memorial park, mannequins of guerillas lie on straw mats in their sleeping quarters, or are assembled around a table for a Party meeting. They stand in a newsroom, facing a chalkboard bulletin, awaiting news and instructions. Inside the tunnels, life-sized wax figures dressed in hospital scrubs bend over an emergency surgery procedure. Others are huddled beside a meeting table underneath a banner inscribed with a common slogan: "Nothing is more precious than freedom" ("*Không có gì quý hơn độc lập, tự do*").

There are live actors dressed as guerillas, each performing a single task, such as kneeling to uproot grass stalks in the swamp or plunging a fishing net into the water. They repeat these actions all day, until the park closes, blending with the visitors in the imitation landscape. It is difficult to discern who is a part of the reenactment.

It astonishes me that, despite the ways my family personally suffered under the Communists, they still revere them. Maybe what they respect is the commitment and devotion. Once, my grandmother asked me if I knew that Uncle Ho never had a family. The nation was his family, she explained with a tone of approval. "He saw all of us as a family. He left Vietnam to train in France then in Russia, but he knew he would return. Thirty years later he came back. For thirty years he kept us in his heart."

My grandmother could no longer walk, and the park's paths were too narrow for a wheelchair. My aunt and uncle carried her through the site. In their devoted hands, she flew.

I recalled my family's trip to the tunnels to X one night as we sat at a dim bar in our neighborhood in Hanoi, full of alleys that fold into each other, tucking us into the city. Like many businesses in the area, the bar is owned by Korean expats. I recounted to X that while walking in the memorial park, I had come upon an old billboard in the middle of a grassy expanse. The billboard depicted a guerilla fighter carrying a baby with a gun strapped to her body in a buoyant swoop; the text below her read, "Go to battle to claim the spring" ("*Ra trận để giành lấy mùa xuân*"). There's an eros of propagation to the phrase: acts of resistance refigured as symbols of fecundity.

X pulled out his phone and began typing in the search bar. He showed me one of Hồ Chí Minh's New Year's poems, written before the Fall of Saigon, about aspirations to reunite the country. It was written in participatory tense. We huddled together to read the screen.

> The South is like root and branches,
> Blood brothers, fighting with one heart.
> Then there was a successful unification,
> North and South, we are happy together again.
> A few kind words,
> It's both a call and a celebration of spring.

> *Nam như cội với cành,*
> *Anh em ruột thịt, đấu tranh một lòng.*
> *Rồi đây thống nhất thành công,*
> *Bắc Nam ta lại vui chung một nhà.*
> *Mấy lời thân ái nôm na,*
> *Vừa là kêu gọi, vừa là mừng xuân.*

The things I learned from X felt strangely innate, like what I had always known but forgotten.

"You know Hanoi used to be named Vạn Xuân, back in the sixth century," he told me that night. "You know what Vạn means, don't you?" I shook my head. "Ten thousand. Ten thousand Springs."

VI

On my last night in Hanoi, X came over to my apartment. When he rang the bell, it was nearly midnight.
I was leaving for the airport at dawn and had been
lying awake for several hours, hounded by dread.
I pulled an oversized T-shirt over my head.

X stood in the doorway, backlit from the
hallway light, holding up a bottle before moving inside.
I asked him how he was and didn't hear what he said.
We looked at my suitcases standing upright by the wall.

Two of them contained all the materials I had
gathered on Vietnamese history—books and scans
from my research trip that I would now take home,
to the heart of the empire that had decimated this city.
I planned to scrutinize these stories from a distance,
to stitch together some semblance of a lineage.

X looked disappointed. Maybe he was just sad
I was leaving, or maybe the disappointment ran deeper.
He couldn't fly off with me and he would never
write this story. I was the one with the passport and
suitcases. The diasporist is also just a tourist in the end.

I brought two glasses from the kitchen as we
went into the bedroom. I lowered myself onto the
bed while he stood over me, unscrewing the bottle.
In the dark he sat down on a chair facing me. I could
hear the neighbors playing ABBA's "Happy New Year"
outside my window, a song all Vietnamese people
know. *May we all have our hopes, our will to try, if we
don't, we might as well lay down and die . . .*

We remained in the same position for hours, mostly in silence. The night sky, illuminated by pollution and LEDs, gradually lightened. At dawn, my consciousness flickering, he decided to leave. There wasn't much left to say at that point. Everything was clear.

The Postsocialist Condition

On Nostalgia and Anti-communism in Vietnamese Art

In 2011, an art collective called The Propeller Group (TPG) collaborated with an ad agency called TBWA/ Vietnam to develop a campaign that would "promote a positive brand identity for communism." They produced an elaborate brand identity that could adorn a wide range of products, from tote bags to hard hats. The art-project-as-media-campaign culminated in a faux-promotional video called *Television Commercial for Communism*.

A conspicuously multiracial cast in white clothing inhabited a staged white environment, surrounded by furniture and trees made from cutout paper. In one frame, members of a nuclear family nod at one another across a dining room table; in another, a man strums his guitar in performed bliss while gazing into the distance. The live-action scenes are mixed with an animated world of equally cheery stock characters who carry colorful crescent shapes. "We all make the same living . . . share all the world . . . live as one and speak the language of smiles," a voice-over says. The characters hold up their crescents—the smiles— to one another and join them to form a huge circle. This circle then morphs into a flag at full mast, underwritten by the caption "This is the new communism."

This video was exhibited in the 2012 New Museum Triennial, *The Ungovernables*, in the Guggenheim's 2013 exhibition *No Country: Contemporary Art for South and Southeast Asia*, and later as part of TPG's solo exhibition *The Propeller Group* at the Museum of Contemporary Art in Chicago in 2016. According to TPG members Tuan Andrew Nguyen, Phunam, and Matt Lucero, the project drew on input from a focus group they had organized, which included "a range of views, from a Chinese American, Vietnamese American, Vietnamese, Indonesian, Indian, and a Tibetan." The one Tibetan participant, Tsering Tashi Gyalthang, was reportedly skeptical, having faced repression from the Chinese government. "Of course, we weren't promoting the ideology of communism," TPG summarized their response to him. "Rather, we [were] exploring its relationship to capitalist ideology in the form of the television commercial, which we think nods to a larger global shift in the marketplace today." Gyalthang found this answer reassuring and agreed to work with TPG as a video director, contributing decisions that became central to the final work. He decided, for example, that the actors would stand entirely still as the camera panned around them, rendering them in contrived states of joy. "Seeing the actors immobile," a TPG member elaborated, "with big smiles, captured these comments of happiness and 'humanism' promised by the communism in the commercial—and it made that communist dream of happiness seem slightly perverse."

TPG was indeed responding to a perverted social contract. Though it is still called the Communist Party, the body that governs Vietnam today can hardly be regarded as committed to communism in practice. When exactly the regime began to depart from Marxist-

Leninist doctrine is a matter of dispute—whether it was after the North's takeover during the Fall of Saigon after 1975, or perhaps even earlier, during the Việt Minh's consolidation of power after the 1945 August Revolution. The particular dissonance that *Television Commercial for Communism* highlights is life after the 1986 economic reforms known as "Đổi Mới" ("renovation" or "innovation"), which transformed the country into a market socialist economy.

After failed prior attempts, the Đổi Mới reforms successfully reconstructed the country's economic system through free-trade policies. After the political resolution of the Third Indochina War and the collapse of the Soviet Union in 1991, the United States lifted its trade embargo on Vietnam in 1994. Following recommendations by the IMF and World Bank, the country privatized its state-owned enterprises after reaching a bilateral trade agreement with the US in 2002 and entered the World Trade Organization in 2007. From 2000 to 2009, the percentage of the population working public sector jobs dropped from 60 to 20 percent, as the workforce underwent what was called "equitization," or the transfer of public assets to the private sector.

Opinions are split on how best to refer to the present period. Some scholars prefer "late socialism," which signals a continuation or direct derivative from prior systems of governance. Less common is the term "postsocialism," which remains a misnomer because the Communist Party still governs and would censor opinions that indicate otherwise. Yet the controversy and baggage of this term—of outdated twentieth-century Cold War dichotomies that still maintain a stronghold on the public imagination—make it more instructive than the more common "late socialism" or "socialism with Vietnamese characteristics."

Vietnam's economic reforms followed China's, which transitioned from an era of centralized planning and collectivization to market socialism under continued single-party rule; in Chinese academic discourse, the term "postsocialism" gained prominence to describe post-Mao state socialism. As film historian Jason McGrath writes about Chinese art and literature in the 1990s:

> in many ways, this postsocialist condition is shared with the societies formerly subsumed under the Soviet Union and its allies and satellite states, in that, despite their differences, all these states were under the rule of Communist parties with their origins in the 1919 Comintern and the Bolshevik model of the "dictatorship of the proletariat."

Historian Artif Dirlik optimistically described postsocialism in 1989 as a "radical vision of the future" that "offers the possibility in the midst of a crisis in socialism of rethinking socialism in new, more creative ways." Yet, following organized communism's chaotic disintegration across Eastern Europe, "postsocialism" was weighed down by an entourage of negative connotations. It's a condition that, as literary theorist

Shu-mei Shih notes, is "constituted in the wake of the failure of twentieth-century revolutionary projects" whose collapse "hastened the onward march toward market economy and neoliberalization, which instituted the liberal humanism of the market as the implicit standard." In this sense then, Shih argues, postsocialism is a nonlocalized condition that not only impacts countries that underwent decommunization, but affects the entire world.

While the Vietnamese independence movement became a major symbol of third world resistance for the global left in the second half of the twentieth century, and today remains a popular historical comparison, there has been markedly less outside interest in what has become of the project. Within Vietnam, these reflections are mediated—or in some cases, chilled—by a government still in possession of its old censorious powers retooled for new aims. This complex conjuncture makes for rich subject matter for contemporary art with all its abstraction. Art made within Vietnam and across its diaspora after 1989 contains postsocialist reflections that are at times nostalgic and ambiguous, at times disenchanted and cynical. Postsocialist art reflects the current dissonance—or perversion—of Vietnamese society; at the same time, it risks contributing to a misrepresentation of the country's complex past and the way Vietnam presently operates.

What is Postsocialist Art?

"Postsocialist art" refers to work made not only in a particular period, but work made possible by specific structural shifts—starting with the opening of communication channels between Vietnam and the rest of the world. It is distinguished by the mixture of private and state funding for artistic production and its networks of distribution. Describing these circumstances as they relate to the film industry, scholar Mariam Lam identifies Nguyễn Võ Nghiêm Minh's 2004 *Buffalo Boy* (*Mùa Len Trâu*) as an unprecedented postsocialist film that was primarily shot in Vietnam but largely funded by external sources—highlighting the ways that state-owned production houses selectively collaborate with private entities and foreign film enterprises to compete in the globalized film industry.

Similar influences were at work in the formation of The Propeller Group as an advertising-adjacent art collective. Members Tuan Andrew Nguyen and Phunam recall:

> We realized that recording in public without government permission was dangerous. Advertisers, on the other hand, were supported and granted access to public spaces. Accordingly, the group opted to incorporate as an advertising company and obtain a film studio license—to be able to film in public spaces and to distribute content via cinemas and television.

The most emphatically postsocialist work directly references Marxist-Leninist aesthetics and culture. One example is *Study of the Fluctuation of a Shadow* (2014) by the Hanoian artist Nguyễn Huy An, a minimalist painting depicting the white outline of a statue of Lenin in Hanoi, and an equation Nguyễn devised through calculating the area of the shadow cast by the statue at three o'clock in the afternoon. Though the sketch is reminiscent of a chalk outline at a murder scene, the descriptive text on the gallery's website remains neutral, simply stating that it is a reflection on "the undeniable significance of Lenin as a political figure in the history of Vietnam . . . and the way our logic, ideals, and world views have always been contained and impacted by natural forces beyond our control." Such an ambiguous description is customary for art exhibited locally, and always hints at an effort to evade the state's stringent censorship of political criticism.

Though the outright position of artists who reference socialist iconography is hard to discern in most cases, some do express nostalgia that verges on sentimentality. In Trần Minh Đức's 2019 exhibition *We Are Happy to Learn to be Stars* at the Factory Contemporary Art Gallery in Ho Chi Minh City, the artist took found photographs of schoolchildren performing the choreographed socialist dance "Pink Lotus" and arranged them on a wall next to a wooden table displaying a collection of Hồ Chí Minh Young Pioneer Organization (Đội Viên) books. Offering instructions on "how to be a young Communist member" ("*quy tắc đoàn đội, trò chơi tập thể, trò chơi đoàn đội*"), the books contained illustrated lessons for schoolchildren seamlessly shifting from "how to tie a red scarf" and "how to move in a group" to "how to salute Uncle Ho." The installation is personal, as Trần told me, building on his childhood spent singing in a similar choir, and reflecting "the belief of a person who is born from a socialist country with all the personal, familial memories."

As part of the exhibition, Trần staged a performance for which he invited schoolgirls to perform a "Pink Lotus" dance. One by one, the schoolgirls came on stage, wearing matching pink uniforms and hair accessories, holding orbs of light. They sang a song called "Counting Star" while performing a static choreography. "People know the big side, the big history," Trần recalled. "These are the little things that I know, the little happier stories that I would share. When the counting star song is performed, it lights up a memory that is inside already, the formation of belief."

Trần's work resonates with what the art historian Chang Tan has termed "communal aesthetics." This refers to art that engages with the communist legacy in China and Mao's slogan "art for the masses," revisiting how incumbent ideologies were felt and lived. These reenactments commemorate personal and collective experiences, searching this legacy for an alternate methodology that "explores the communal aspect of art—to create, no matter how fleetingly, an aesthetic utopia where the joy of discovery, expression and creativity is integrated with everyday life."

Communal art, Tan writes, is impossible to reproduce because its source materials are primarily individual memories. Even "being there" does not guarantee participation; the performance activates the shared knowledge and experiences that are particular to a community.

Another work that revisits the country's socialist history with surprising ambiguity is Vietnamese American artist Hương Ngô's *In the Shadow of the Future* (2019). The mixed-media architectural installation references the communal housing structures designed by Jean Renaudie and Renée Gailhoustet in Ivry-sur-Seine, one of Paris's so-called *banlieues rouges* (red suburbs), where many Vietnamese refugees settled. Placed within a wooden trilateral sculpture modeled after the star-shaped, terraced housing complexes, three monitors display videos of a cosmonaut loitering in the neighborhood and interacting with local French union members. The protagonist is based on Phạm Tuân, a Vietnamese fighter pilot who became the first Asian space traveler in 1980 when he went into orbit with the Soviet Intercosmos program as part of the USSR's "friendship diplomacy." On the wall hangs a concrete relief of a newspaper clipping that touts the mission's victory for the Communist Party of Vietnam. *In the Shadow of the Future* poignantly imagines the communist spirit persisting in these refugees who fled their country to practice communal living elsewhere. Their journey tracks a continuation of the communist tradition, one that is both diasporic and disentangled from the nation-state.

Yet what characterizes most postsocialist art is not the continuity but the break—the legacy of Đổi Mới. In 1994, the year Bill Clinton lifted the trade embargo on Vietnam, a *New York Times* article reports, "Pepsico imported the first Pepsi-Cola flavor concentrate and began distributing the drink an hour after the White House announced the end of the trade ban."

A popped bottle overflowing with pent-up fizz is a decent metaphor for the arrival of contemporary art. In a catalog for the exhibition *Uncorked Soul*— held at Plum Blossoms Gallery in Hong Kong in 1991— art critic Jeffrey Hantover compares Đổi Mới to reform movements such as glasnost and perestroika. Hantover quotes a Vietnamese artist who declared that, thanks to the transition, "originality and diversity had begun to replace the monotony of the collective." As art historians Nora Taylor and Pamela Corey observe, "In the early 1990s, it was as if all writing on art centered on this image, the allegory of the once repressed and now suddenly free, liberated, and liberal Vietnam."

While Taylor and Corey question whether the adoption of a market economy in Vietnam translated into a radical refashioning of the arts, it is clear that art after Đổi Mới rejected depictions of collectivity, which now bore the signs of the "old repressive and autocratic regime." Postsocialist art is thus distinguished by this burst of subjectivity signaling the end of a period of repression. The crude dichotomy between collective conservatism and individualistic freedom of expression has long been enforced by the state. After the Việt Minh's victory and the formation of the Cultural Association for National Salvation in the 1940s, there were fierce debates among Marxist intellectuals about the relationship between politics and aesthetics. By the 1950s, the Party implemented restrictive guidelines for artistic production. Socialist art was defined against an enemy—the perceived bourgeois decadence of the West. Take Hồ Chí Minh's famous response to an exhibition at the Cultural Association for National Salvation in 1945: "All these paintings are very beautiful but these are upper-class beauties. Why don't you make paintings about lower-class beauties around us?" Similarly, in Trường Chinh's 1949 "Marxism and Vietnamese Culture," the general secretary of the Communist Party denounced "cubism, expressionism, and avant-garde art forms" as "sprouted from the rotten wood of imperialist culture." Postsocialist art is, then, a reaction to a reaction.

Contradiction

In 2006, The Propeller Group member Tuan Andrew Nguyen (who has built a successful solo career following TPG's official retirement in 2016) created *Proposals for a Vietnamese Landscape*, a series of paintings made in collaboration with Ngô Dong, a painter who formerly worked for the Party. One work in the series, of a sidewalk in Saigon, features a large poster advertisement for Yamaha, where a young woman, sporting jeans and a leather jacket, straddles her new motorbike. Foregrounding what seems to be a spacious vacation house surrounded by palm trees, she's positioned in a low-angle shot so the viewer looks up at her, her grandiosity befitting her aspirations and potential. The sign reads, "Yamaha New! Pop! Classico! Yamaha Pop Mới." Directly below the advertisement is a socialist realist poster in which a group of people face a manufacturing plant in unison as a celestial hammer and sickle casts light over their faces. That text reads, "The spirit of the Southern resistance war did not die." ("*Tinh thần ngày nam bộ kháng chiến bất diệt.*")

The painting evokes competing notions of "the good life," where people are "drawn into competitive striving and the accumulation of private wealth to keep up with market demands, even as the socialist ethos of harmony, equality, and mutuality persist in official and popular discourse." Both the advertisement and the mobilization poster depict performative happiness, though the former increasingly feels more realist than the latter. Put up decades before, the mobilization poster is faded, looking as outworn as its ideas. The glossy advertisement, in contrast, offers a glimpse of a modern lifestyle: freedom expressed through consumerism and economic prosperity. As this novel modern fantasy increasingly manifests in young city dwellers, and old nationalist signifiers fade, communist disenchantment becomes further cemented.

Nguyen states that the paintings in the series attempt to "capture the conflicted visual terrain," where the landscape reveals

> a waged battle between socialist propaganda and capitalist marketing strategies . . . Working in media and advertising has given us a vantage point from which we can explore the strategies involved in the creation and widespread dissemination of ideas. And it's not much different than propaganda.

Thirty years after Đổi Mới, this tendency has remained popular among Vietnamese and diaspora artists. The most prominent recent example may be Vietnamese American artist Diane Severin Nguyen's first solo institutional exhibition *IF REVOLUTION IS A SICKNESS* (2021) at SculptureCenter in New York. The film component of the show begins with an orphaned Vietnamese girl who washes ashore in Poland. Years later, isolated in Warsaw, she is taken in by a South Korean K-pop dance group. She later appears on-screen in a yellow shirt with red sleeves reminiscent of the Vietnamese flag. As the didactic text elaborates, "K-pop is used by the artist as a vernacular material to trace a relationship between Eastern Europe and Asia with roots in Cold War allegiances."

To cast these dancers, Nguyen scoured Instagram for K-pop cover groups in Poland and connected with dancers such as Jakub Grzybała, a rising star and member of Majesty Dance Team. Nguyen also found the main character, Weronika (one of the most common Polish names), by searching "Weronika Nguyen." The piece functions as a high-concept music video that blends disparate charged imagery and references, from the dancers' goth sportswear to the Stalinist architecture behind their dance sequences. In the film, gold foil balloons spell out the year 1989.

After practicing dance moves in an abandoned factory, Weronika sits on a bridge overlooking a river and wonders aloud, "Where is there a beautiful surface without its terrible depth?" Weronika's question encapsulates Nguyen's postmodern approach to artmaking, stringing together unlikely imagery and sources—from Britney Spears lyrics to quotes by Hannah Arendt, Édouard Glissant, Mao Zedong, and Ulrike Meinhof—through loose associative logic. In a talk at SculptureCenter, Nguyen explained that she was interested in thinking about the coercive image-making aspects of both communism and capitalism. The mix of disjointed symbolism—from the autotune pop songs to the dreary Soviet monuments—exemplifies postsocialist art techniques, which Tan describes as "employed to create a sense of irony. The past is invoked as an awkward juxtaposition of icons and cliches, so that it may be revealed as incoherent, deceptive and fragmentary."

Nguyen's exhibition demonstrates the similarities between the aesthetic tendencies of postmodernity and postsocialism, not only in the dissociated ways images and symbols circulate, but also in how both generally favor the discursive over the ideological. "What emerged in the ruins of the USSR and its protégés," Tan writes, "was the destructive glee of postmodernism, which is essentially a reaction to utopianism." This destructive glee recalls what Stuart Hall described as "the postmodern argument about the implosion of the real." But what may we conclude from the central postmodern contention that there is no fixed meaning and that all realities are fragmented? To echo Hall's concern, "there is all the difference in the world between the assertion that there is no one, final, absolute meaning—no ultimate signified, only the endlessly sliding chain of signification, and on the other hand, the assertion that meaning does not exist."

What Happens After the End?

"This is the end of history," a voice-over seductively whispers in the final moments of the film *IF REVOLUTION IS A SICKNESS*. Following an ecstatic parade of discordant mashups, this declaration evokes not only Fukuyama but, for me, Hall's description of postmodernism as a trap, an endless present: "all you can do is be with it, immersed in it." Originally expressed in 1986, Hall's cautions against nihilism bear repeating today:

> You can live this as a metaphor, suggesting that certain contemporary positions and ideas are now deeply undermined, rendered increasingly fragile as it were, by having the fact of the world's end as one of their imminent possibilities. That is a radically new historical fact and, I think, it has decentered us all.

Postsocialist art shares postmodernist art's aversion to ideology, equating strong beliefs—whether it be consumerist desire or political conviction—with indoctrination. In perpetually equating capitalism and communism as equally coercive, what is the effective thrust of postsocialist art? Per Hall, where can we go once we've established that the positions we've inherited have been deeply undermined?

    After opening at SculptureCenter in 2021, *IF REVOLUTION IS A SICKNESS* traveled and was reproduced for the Renaissance Society in Chicago and the Contemporary Art Museum in Houston. Like *Television Commercial for Communism*, these presentations were met with resounding press acclaim. Virtuosic artistry notwithstanding, such glowing reception nonetheless raises the question: What exactly does the art world, or the American art-going public, find so resonant in works that caricaturize the communist legacy, in an era when working-class power has been thoroughly weakened?

A cynic might conjecture that postsocialist art functions as a provocative trend, as a type of red tourism within contemporary art. Art that is critical of state communism also comfortably aligns with the anti-communist liberalism that was so foundational to US postwar art, a history that feels both belabored and willfully forgotten. When in 1954 the chairman of MoMA's board, August Heckscher, declared the museum's work "related to the struggle of freedom against tyranny," when Eisenhower designated MoMA as a government proxy, and when the CIA founded the Congress for Cultural Freedom, Communism was at the peak of its global appeal. This is, of course, no longer the case. Postsocialist art, as Tan writes, "not only overlooks the irreducible differences between Modernist and Communist discourse, but also fails to reach a fair assessment of the Communist legacy— as both a theoretical speculation and a political entity." Art that propagates this view reduces Vietnam's diverse revolutionary heritage to state actions. It also removes Vietnam from the context of the international

97   The Postsocialist Condition

development of socialism, which in many cases was integrated with the civil rights and anticolonial movements of the global 1960s.

If postsocialist critique is reductive, individual artists and curators are not the sole culprits—nor are MoMA, the Guggenheim, or other US cultural institutions. The Communist Party of Vietnam has itself perpetuated a distorted version of its own history, erasing vibrant internal debates and silencing opposition to state Communism, whether from within a Marxist framework or not. Postsocialist art vividly reflects the strange mutations undergone by the current Party, which has drastically departed from, yet still appeals to, its Communist identity. It remains important to inquire, at each instance, whether the appropriation of state-socialist iconography illuminates the present's relationship with the past or obfuscates it further.

PREFACE

Bharath, Deepa. "Vietnamese Artists' Exhibit Shut Down by Threat of Protests." *Orange County Register*, January 16, 2009. https://www .ocregister.com/2009/01/16/vietnamese-artists-exhibit-shut-down-by -threat-of-protests/.

Coburn, Judith. "The Girl in the Photograph." *Los Angeles Times*, August 20, 1989.

Nguyen, Mimi Thi. *The Gift of Freedom: War, Debt, and Other Refugee Passages*. Durham: Duke University Press, 2012.

RED CITY SMART CITY

Gibert, Marie, and Peyvel, Emmanuelle. "The Reshaping of Post-Socialist Ho Chi Minh City: Leisure Practices and Social Control." In *Socialist and Post-Socialist Urbanisms: Critical Reflections from a Global Perspective*, edited by Lisa B.W. Drummond and Douglas Young, 143–61. Toronto: University of Toronto Press, 2020.

Reed, John. "The Rise and Rise of a Vietnamese Corporate Empire." *Financial Times*, June 26, 2019. https://www.ft.com/content/84323c32 -9799-11e9-9573-ee5cbb98ed36.

Schwenkel, Christina. *Building Socialism: The Afterlife of East German Architecture in Urban Vietnam*. Durham: Duke University Press, 2020.

CULTURE POLICE

Butt, Zoe. "Red Tape and Digital Talismans: Shaping Knowledge Beneath Surveillance." In *Art in the Asia-Pacific: Intimate Publics*, edited by Larissa Hjorth, Natalie King, and Mami Kataoka, 91–104. London: Routledge, 2014.

Butt, Zoe, and Dinh Q. Lê. "Presentation about Sàn Art by Zoe Butt and Dinh Q Le." *Asia Art Archive in America*, June 21, 2010. https://www.aaa-a.org/programs/presentation-by-zoe-butt-and-dinh-q-le.

Butt, Zoe, Bill Nguyen, and Le Thien Bao. "Spirit of Friendship: Artist Groups in Vietnam Since 1975." *Southeast of Now: Directions in Contemporary and Modern Art in Asia* 2, no. 1 (March 2018): 145–79.

Lê, Linh. "Art and Cultural Censorship in Vietnam: An Ever-Changing Terrain." *ArtsEquator*, September 6, 2023. https://artsequator.com/art-and-cultural-censorship-in-vietnam-an-ever-changing-terrain/.

Libby, Samantha. "The Art of Censorship in Vietnam." *Journal of International Affairs* 65, no. 1 (Fall/Winter 2011): 209–218.

MY NORTH VIETNAMESE FRIEND

Bảo Ninh. *The Sorrow of War: A Novel of North Vietnam*. Translated by Phan Thanh Hao. New York: Riverhead Books, 1996.

Đặng, Thai Mai. *Văn học khái luận* [An outline of literature]. Hanoi: Hàn Thuyên, 1944.

Feuerbach, Ludwig. *The Essence of Christianity*. Translated by George Eliot. Amherst: Prometheus Books, 2008.

Fuller, John. "Bao Ninh's Wars." *Mekong Review* 3, no. 12 (August 2018): 12–15.

Hồ, Chí Minh. *New Year's Poems*. Hanoi: Foreign Languages Publishing House, 1979.

Hình Ảnh Việt-Nam [Vietnam pictorial], no. 18 (February 1957).

Inani, Rohit. "The Long Silence of Bao Ninh." *Diacritics*, December 14, 2018. https://dvan.org/2018/12/the-long-silence-of-bao-ninh/.

Lam Điền. "Điện ảnh bưng biền không thể 'nằm ngoài lịch sử'" [Bưng Biền cinema cannot be outside of history]. *Tuổi Trẻ Online*, October 4, 2010. https://tuoitre.vn/dien-anh-bung-bien-khong-the-nam-ngoai-lich-su-372765.htm.

Lotz, Christian. "Against Essentialist Conceptions of Love: Towards a Social-Materialist Conception of Love." In *Thinking About Love: Essays in Contemporary Continental Philosophy*, edited by Dianne Enns, 131–48. University Park: Penn State University Press, 2015.

Marcuse, Herbert. *Eros and Civilization: A Philosophical Inquiry into Freud*. Boston: Beacon Press, 1955.

Marx, Karl. "Theses on Feuerbach." In *Collected Works of Karl Marx and Friedrich Engels*, vol. 5, *1845–1847*. London: Lawrence & Wishart, 1976.

Nguyễn, Đình Thi. "Tìm nghĩa hiện thực mới" [Seeking the meaning of the new realism]. *Văn Nghệ*, no. 10 (March 1949): 2.

Nguyễn, Tuân. "Cách mạng, kháng chiến và đời sống văn học (1945–1954)" [Revolution, resistance, and the literary life]. *Viện Văn Học* 3 (1995).

Nguyen, Qui-Ha Hoang. "Cinema of Care: The Child Figure, the Collective, and War in 'The Little Girl of Ha Noi.'" *Feminist Media Histories* 9, no. 1 (2023): 33–51.

Ninh Kim N. B. *A World Transformed: The Politics of Culture in Revolutionary Vietnam, 1945–1965*. Ann Arbor: University of Michigan Press, 2002.

Phu, Thy. *Warring Visions: Photography and Vietnam*. Durham: Duke University Press, 2021.

Schwenkel, Christina. *Building Socialism: The Afterlife of East German Architecture in Urban Vietnam*. Durham: Duke University Press, 2020.

Tô, Ngọc Vân. "Học Hay Không Học?" [Study or Not?]. *Văn Nghệ*, no. 10 (March 1949): 3–4.

Tô, Ngọc Vân. "Vẫn Tranh Tuyên Truyền Và Hội Họa" [Still on propaganda paintings and art]. *Văn Nghệ*, no. 2 (April–May 1948): 5–6.

Browne, Malcolm W. "First US Trade Exhibit Is Held in Hanoi." *New York Times*, April 24, 1994.

Corey, Pamela, and Nora Taylor. "Đổi Mới and the Globalization of Vietnamese Art." *Journal of Vietnamese Studies* 14, no. 2 (Winter 2019): 1–34.

Dirlik, Arif. "Postsocialism? Reflections on Socialism with Chinese Characteristics." *Critical Asian Studies* 21, no. 1 (March 1989): 33–44.

Hall, Stuart. "On Postmodernism and Disarticulation: An Interview with Stuart Hall by Larry Grossberg." In Stuart Hall, *Essential Essays*, vol. 1, *Foundations of Cultural Studies*, edited by David Morley, 223–42. Durham: Duke University Press, 2018.

Lam, Mariam. "Circumventing Channels: Indie Filmmaking in Post-Socialist Việt Nam and Beyond." In *Glimpses of Freedom: Independent Cinema in Southeast Asia*, edited by May Ingawanij and Benjamin McKay, 96–107. Ithaca: Cornell University Press, 2012.

McGrath, Jason. *Postsocialist Modernity: Chinese Cinema, Literature, and Criticism in the Market Age*. Stanford: Stanford University Press, 2008.

Mehta, Diane. "Interview: The Propeller Group." *BOMB Magazine*, February 21, 2013. https://bombmagazine.org/articles/20.

Nguyen, Diane Severin. "Diane Severin Nguyen: *IF REVOLUTION IS A SICKNESS*." SculptureCenter. https://www.sculpture-center.org/exhibitions/13184/if-revolution-is-a-sickness.

Nguyen, Minh T. N., Phill Wilcox, and Jake Lin. "The Good Life in Late-Socialist Asia: Aspirations, Politics, and Possibilities." *Positions* 32, no. 1 (February 2024): 1–18.

Nguyen, Tuan Andrew. "Proposals for a Vietnamese Landscape." https://www.tuanandrewnguyen.com/proposalsforavietnameselandscape.

Shih, Shu-mei. "Is the Post- in Postsocialism the Post- in Posthumanism?" *Social Text* 30, no. 1 (March 2012): 27–50.

Tan, Chang. "Art for/of the Masses." *Third Text* 26, no. 2 (2012): 177–94.

Acknowledgements

It is a privilege and blessing that for this book I was able to work with a team who understood me and cared about the project. I'm grateful to my editor Léon Dische Becker, who refined every idea and every line in these pages; my designer Bryce Wilner for treating the process as artistic collaboration; and my copy editor Andreas Petrossiants for the discerning review. Deep thanks to all at Wendy's Subway and Art Metropole, especially Rachel Valinsky for the steadying support and Blair Swann for the trust from the very beginning.

This book directly and indirectly benefited from Fogo Island Arts, the Andy Warhol Arts Writers Grant, and Asia Art Archive's "Art Schools of Asia" seminar. I'm grateful to KUNCI School of Improper Education (especially Rifki Akbar Pratama, and by extension, Harry Burke) in Jogja for the invitation to workshop what would become "Culture Police," and to Á Space (especially Vân Đỗ) in Hanoi for the invitation to present what would become "The Postsocialist Condition," first published in *e-flux journal* in October 2024. Special thanks to Shiv Kotecha and Pradeep Dalal for the invitation to write "My North Vietnamese Friend," which was first published for Cookie Jar, the Andy Warhol Arts Writers Grant's pamphlet series.

I am indebted to Hoàng Mai at Vietnam Film Institute and to Nguyễn Ngân for helping me in the archive and accompanying me to Vinh. My gratitude also goes to Nguyễn Ngọc Liên for all the cultural translation; Dominic Scriven for research opportunities; Thuy-Han Nguyen-Chi for travel companionship; Dr. Jennifer Dorothy Lee for the formative seminars on Asian art and revolutions; and Jacobo Zambrano-Rangel for being my home on earth.

Writing is thinking, and neither are ever done alone. I owe much to friends who read earlier drafts: David Borgonjon, Mimi Howard, and Vũ Minh Hoàng. These texts were also meaningfully influenced by Matt Browning, Zoe Butt, Olivia Crough, Jane DeBevoise, Emily Dhatt, Đỗ Tường Linh, Peter Goldberg, Nasrin Himada, Jason Hirata, Imani Elizabeth Jackson, Leena Joshi, Lê Thiên-Bảo, Linh Lê, Farid Mattar, Soledad Fátima Muñoz, Quyên Nguyễn-Hoàng, Grace Nissan, Marcel Purnell, Asha Ransby-Sporn, Alexander Si, Nora Taylor, Arlette Quỳnh-Anh Trần, and Trần Duy Hưng.

This book is written in memory of the late Sàn Art founder Dinh Q Lê, and dedicated to the Hai Bà Trưng School for Organizing (especially Phuong T Vuong, Thuan Nguyen, and Hải Võ).

Last, thank you to my family, whose love made me real.

Memorial Park: Revisiting Vietnam
© 2025 Minh Nguyen

First Edition, 2025
Edition of 1,250 copies
ISBN: 978-1-989010-33-4
US Library of Congress Control
Number (LCCN): 2025940831
Cataloguing in Publication (CIP)
information is available from
Library and Archives Canada

Edited by Léon Dische Becker
Copy edited by Andreas Petrossiants
Proofread by Rachel Valinsky
Designed by Bryce Wilner
Typeset in Garamond No. 8 and
    Geometric No. 3.5
Printed at Grafiche Veneziane, Italy

Cover: Still from Đặng Nhật Minh,
When the Tenth Month Comes
(*Bao giờ cho đến tháng Mười*), 1984
pp. 113–44: Photographs by Minh
Nguyen, 2019–2024

Published by Art Metropole and
    Wendy's Subway

Art Metropole
896 College Street
Toronto, ON M6H 1A4
Canada
artmetropole.com

Art Metropole is a non-profit
artist-run centre that publishes,
promotes, exhibits, archives,
and distributes artists' books,
multiples, and related media.

Wendy's Subway
379 Bushwick Avenue
Brooklyn, NY 11206
United States of America
wendyssubway.com

Wendy's Subway is a non-profit
reading room, writing space, and
independent publisher located
in Brooklyn.

Distributed in Canada
by Art Metropole
artmetropole.com

Distributed in the USA
by Asterism Books
asterismbooks.com

Distributed in Europe/the UK
by Antenne Books
antennebooks.com

Art Metropole gratefully
acknowledges ongoing support
from the Canada Council for the
Arts, the Ontario Arts Council,
the City of Toronto through
the Toronto Arts Council, as well
as our members and donors.
We also extend our thanks to Fogo
Island Arts, which supported
Minh Nguyen's participation in
The Islands Art Writing Residency.

Wendy's Subway publications are
supported, in part, by the New
York State Council on the Arts
with support of the Office of
the Governor and the New York
State Legislature; and the Mellon
Foundation, via the Coalition
of Small Arts NYC (CoSA).

RA TRẬN ĐỂ GIÀNH LẤY MÙA XUÂN

"Go to battle to claim the spring"

↑ Plate 12   Larger and sturdier *cơi nới* in block C3 display stratification, 2011. Photo by the author.

"This way to the red address"

↑ Plate 12   Larger and sturdier *cối nồi* in block C3 display stratification, 2011. Photo by the author.

"Study - learn more - learn forever
—Lenin"

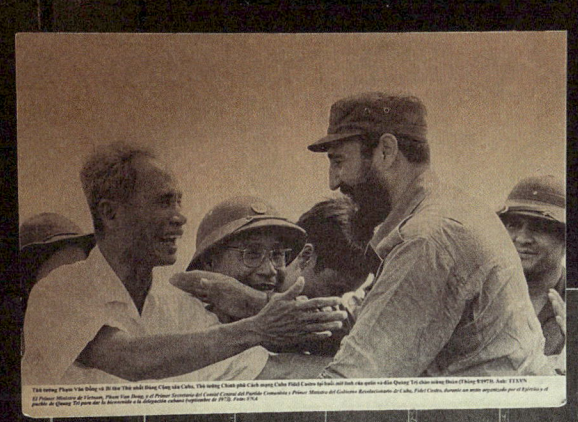

Thủ tướng Phạm Văn Đồng và Bí thư Thứ nhất Đảng Cộng sản Cuba, Thủ tướng Chính phủ Cách mạng Cuba Fidel Castro tại buổi mít tinh của quân và dân Quảng Trị chào mừng Đoàn (Tháng 9/1973). Ảnh: TTXVN

El Primer Ministro de Vietnam, Phạm Văn Đồng, y el Primer Secretario del Comité Central del Partido Comunista y Primer Ministro del Gobierno Revolucionario de Cuba, Fidel Castro, durante un mitin organizado por el Ejército y el pueblo de Quảng Trị para dar la bienvenida a la delegación cubana (septiembre de 1973). Foto: VNA

POR VIETNAM
ESTAMOS DISPUESTOS
A DAR HASTA NUESTRA
PROPIA SANGRE

VÌ VIỆT NAM,
CUBA SẴN SÀNG HIẾN DÂNG
CẢ MÁU CỦA MÌNH!

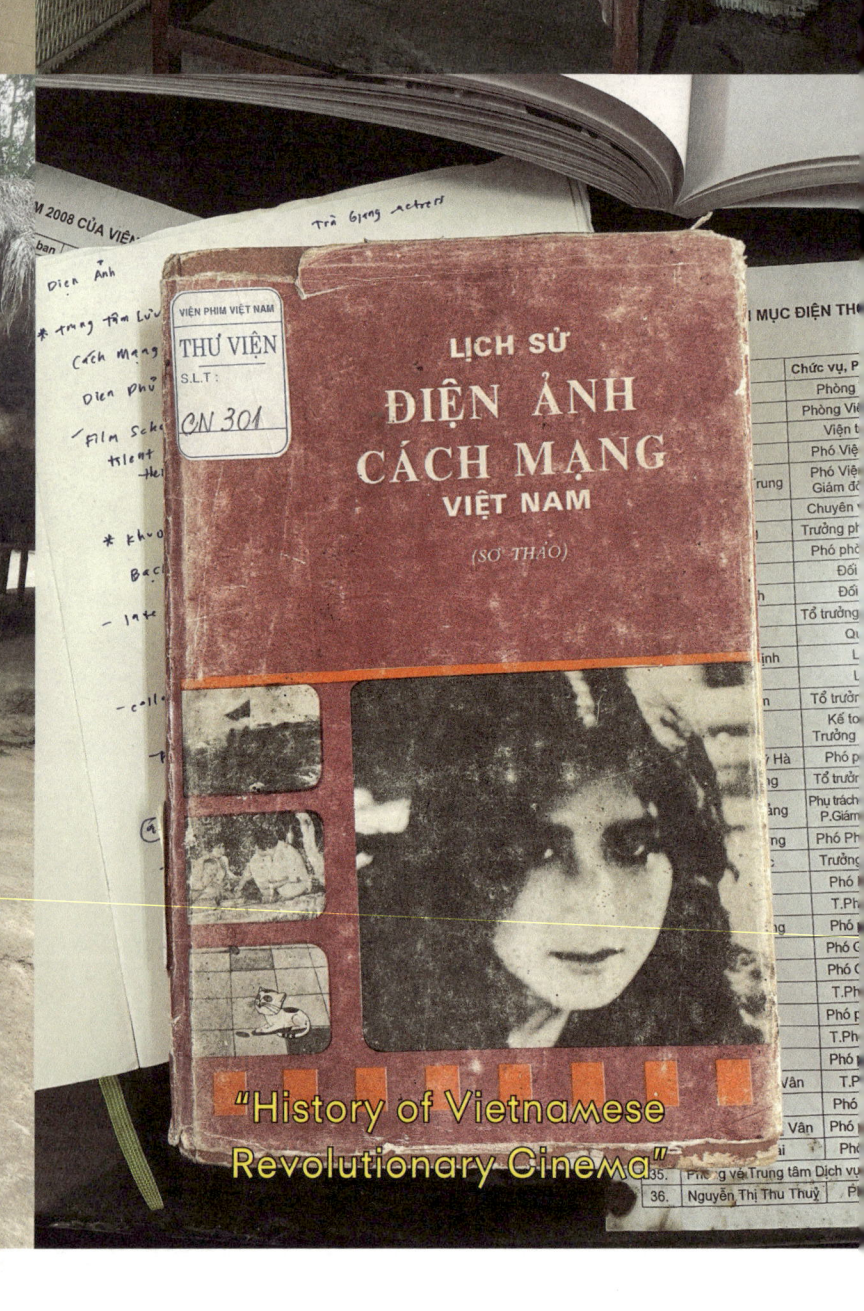

"History of Vietnamese Revolutionary Cinema"